PECAN BREAKFAST COOKBOOK

*"**Your Kitchen Assistant**"*, for Beginners Eager

to Wow Friends and Family

with **Pecan Breakfasts**.

- *Wyatt Brown* -

Table of Contents

1. PUMPKIN PANCAKES WITH SALTED PECAN BUTTERSCOTCH 10
2. CARROT & PECAN MUFFINS 14
3. DATE & BUCKWHEAT GRANOLA WITH PECANS & SEEDS 16
4. CINNAMON PECAN STICKY BUNS 19
5. EASY BANANA PANCAKES 22
6. APPLE MUFFINS WITH PECAN TOPPING............................. 24
7. VEGAN BREAKFAST MUFFINS 27
8. MONKEY BREAD 29
9. BANANA PANCAKES.. 33
10. HOMEMADE MUESLI WITH OATS, DATES & BERRIES............. 35
11. EASY BANANA MUFFINS 37
13. FEEL-GOOD MUFFINS 39
14. PECAN BANANA BREAD.. 41
15. PECAN, GINGER AND DRIED APPLE GRANOLA 45
16. SUPERFOOD PECAN ENERGY BARS 47
17. PECAN COFFEE CAKE OVERNIGHT OATS............................ 49
18. PECAN SUPER SEED CRUMBLE OVERNIGHT OATS 52
19. GREEN APPLE PECAN SMOOTHIE 55
20. MAPLE PECAN OVERNIGHT OATS 57
21. PECAN BUTTER.. 59
22. TOASTED OAT AND PECAN SMOOTHIE 61
23. HONEY PECAN BERRY YOGURT PARFAIT........................... 63
24. BANANA PECAN CHERRY OATMEAL................................. 65
25. BERRY PECAN SMOOTHIE BOWL 67
26. PECAN AND PEACH YOGURT MUFFINS.............................. 69
27. SPICED CITRUS PECAN BREAKFAST BREAD 72
28. WHOLE WHEAT PECAN BANANA MUFFINS 75
29. PECAN AND VEGGIE MINI FRITTATAS................................ 77
30. CHUNKY CHOCOLATE CHIP PECAN BREAKFAST COOKIES 80
31. PECAN PIE BAKED OATMEAL.. 82

32. BAKED FRENCH TOAST WITH PECAN CRUMBLE....................85
33. EXTRA STICKY MAPLE PECAN STICKY BUNS.........................88
34. SHEET PAN EGGS WITH PECAN BREAKFAST "SAUSAGE".........92
35. BREAKFAST BREAD PUDDING WITH PECAN CRUMBLE............95
36. PECAN PROTEIN PANCAKES 98
37. GLUTEN-FREE MAPLE PECAN DONUTS 100

1.   Pumpkin Pancakes with Salted Pecan Butterscotch

Prep: 20 mins

Cook: 25 mins, plus cooling

Easy

Serves 4

INGREDIENTS:

- 250g pumpkin or squash, peeled, deseeded and chopped into large chunks
- 2 eggs
- 3 tbsp light brown soft sugar
- 25g butter, melted, plus a little for cooking
- 125ml buttermilk (or use the same quantity of milk, with a squeeze of lemon juice)
- 200g plain flour
- 2½ tsp baking powder
- 1 tsp ground cinnamon
- drizzle of flavour less oil, such as sunflower or groundnut, for frying
- ice cream, to serve, or yogurt or crème fraîche

For the salted pecan butterscotch:

- 50g pecans, roughly chopped
- 50g butter

- 50g light brown soft sugar
- 1 tsp sea salt flakes
- 100ml double cream

METHOD

1. Put the pumpkin or squash in a large heatproof bowl, add 1 tbsp water, cover with cling film and microwave on High for 5-8 mins or until really soft – different types will take a varying amount of time. Drain the pumpkin well and cool completely. If you want to eat the pancakes for breakfast, this step is best done the night before.

2. Once cool, put the pumpkin in a food processer with the remaining pancake ingredients and add a good pinch of salt. Blend until everything is well combined to a smooth, thick batter (alternatively, mash the pumpkin well, then whisk in the remaining ingredients). Transfer to a jug or piping bag and set aside while you make the butterscotch sauce.

3. Toast the pecans in a saucepan for 1-2 mins until a shade darker. Tip out and set aside. Add the butter, sugar, salt and cream to the pan. Bring to a simmer, then bubble gently for a few mins until you have a shiny sauce. Stir in the pecans and set aside to cool a little.

4. Heat a knob of butter and a drizzle of oil in a large frying pan. Heat oven to 140C/120C fan/gas 1, to keep the pancakes warm while you cook them in batches – have a baking tray to hand. When the butter is foaming, swirl it around the pan, then pour tennis-ball-sized amounts of batter into the pan – they will spread a little as they cook, so leave some space between each pancake and don't overcrowd the pan. Cook over a low-medium heat. Don't touch the pancakes until you see a few bubbles appear on the surface – have a look underneath and, if the pancakes are golden, flip them over and cook for another 2 mins on the other side. Transfer the cooked pancakes to the baking tray and keep warm in the oven while you continue cooking.

5. Once cooked, pile the pancakes onto plates, top with ice cream, yogurt or crème fraîche, and pour over the salted pecan butterscotch sauce.

NUTRITION: per serving

kcal   717

fat   43g

saturates   21g

carbs 68g

sugars   31g

fibre 4g

protein   12g

salt   2.6g

2.   Carrot & Pecan Muffins

Prep:10 mins

Cook:20 mins

Easy

Makes 12

INGREDIENTS:

- 2 x 400g can cannellini beans in water, drained
- 2 tsp ground cinnamon
- 100g porridge oats
- 4 large eggs
- 2 tbsp rapeseed oil
- 4 tbsp maple syrup
- 2 tsp vanilla extract
- zest 1 large orange
- 170g carrot, coarsely grated
- 100g raisins
- 80g pecan halves, 12 reserved, the rest roughly chopped
- 2 tsp baking powder

METHOD

1. Heat oven to 180C/160C fan/gas 4 and line a 12-hole muffin tin with paper cases. Tip the beans into a bowl and add the cinnamon, oats, eggs, oil, maple syrup, vanilla extract and orange zest. Blitz with a hand blender until really smooth – the beans and oats should be ground down as much as possible.

2. Stir in the carrot, raisins, chopped pecans and baking powder, and mix well. Spoon into the muffin cases – use a large ice cream scoop if you have one, to get nice even muffins.

3. Top each muffin with a reserved pecan and bake for 20 mins until set and light brown. Cool on a wire rack. Will keep in the fridge for a few days, or freeze for 6 weeks; thaw at room temperature.

NUTRITION: per serving

low inkcal   209

     fat   9g

     saturates   1g

     carbs 22g

     sugars   11g

     fibre 5g

     protein   7g

     salt   0.3g

3. Date & Buckwheat Granola with Pecans & Seeds

Prep:10 mins

Cook:35 mins, plus overnight soaking

Easy

Serves 8

INGREDIENTS:

For the granola

- 85g buckwheat
- 4 medjool dates , stoned
- 1 tsp ground cinnamon
- 100g traditional oats
- 2 tsp rapeseed oil
- 25g sunflower seeds
- 25g pumpkin seeds
- 25g flaked almonds
- 50g pecan nuts, roughly broken into halves
- 50g sultanas (without added oil)

For the yogurt & fruit (to serve 2)

- 2 x 150ml pots low-fat bio natural yogurt
- 2 ripe nectarines or peaches, stoned and sliced

METHOD

1. Soak the buckwheat overnight in cold water. The next day, drain and rinse the buckwheat. Put the dates in a pan with 300ml water and the cinnamon, and blitz with a stick blender until completely smooth. Add the buckwheat, bring to the boil and cook, uncovered, for 5 mins until pulpy. Meanwhile, heat oven to 150C/130C fan/gas 2 and line two large baking trays with baking parchment.

2. Stir the oats and oil into the date and buckwheat mixture, then spoon small clusters of the mixture onto the baking trays. Bake for 15 mins, then carefully scrape the clusters from the parchment if they have stuck and turn before spreading out again. Return to the oven for another 15 mins, turning frequently, until firm and golden.

3. When the mix is dry enough, tip into a bowl, mix in the seeds and nuts with the sultanas and toss well. When cool, serve each person a generous handful with yogurt and fruit, and pack the excess into an airtight container. Will keep for a week. On other days you can vary the fruit or serve with milk or a dairy-free alternative instead of the yogurt.

NUTRITION: per serving

kcal   387

fat   12g

saturates   2g

carbs 50g

sugars   34g

fibre 3g

protein   15g

salt   0.3g

4. Cinnamon Pecan Sticky Buns

Prep:30 mins

Cook:30 mins

More effort

Serves 8

INGREDIENTS:

- 450g strong white flour
- 50g caster sugar
- 85g butter , cut into small pieces
- 7g sachet dried yeast
- 2 eggs , beaten
- 150ml full-fat milk
- vegetable oil , for greasing

For the filling

- 2 tsp ground cinnamon
- 85g light brown sugar
- 100g pecan

For the topping

- 125g melted butter , plus extra
- 125ml maple syrup
- 50g light brown sugar
- 100g pecan , roughly chopped

METHOD

1. Place the flour, sugar and 1 tsp salt in a mixing bowl, then rub in the pieces of butter until the mix has the texture of breadcrumbs. Tip in the yeast and eggs. Pour in the milk and mix well until you get a soft dough (you may need to add a little more milk). Knead in a mixer with a dough hook for 7 mins or by hand for about 15 mins until the dough is smooth, soft and springy. Tip into a lightly oiled bowl, cover with oiled cling film or a clean tea towel, then leave to rise in a warm place for about 1 hr or until doubled in size.

2. Make the filling: place the cinnamon, sugar and pecans in a food processor, then whizz until the nuts are finely ground. Punch down the dough and knead to knock out the air, then split the dough in two. Roll and stretch each piece to form a 25 x 35cm rectangle.

3. Melt the butter for the topping. Brush half all over each rectangle, then sprinkle half the filling mixture over each. Use a rolling pin to press the filling into the dough. Tightly roll each rectangle up from one of the long ends to get a thick log, then pinch the ends together to seal. Cut each log into 8 pieces. Can be frozen for up to 1 month.

4. Brush two 20 x 30cm deep baking trays with melted butter. Mix the maple syrup and sugar into the remaining butter, then pour this over the bottom of each baking tray, swirling around so it is coated. Sprinkle with the pecans. Place the rolls on the tray, leaving a gap of at least 2cm around each roll. Cover with lightly oiled cling film, then keep in a warm place for about 30 mins until lightly risen.

5. Heat oven to 180C/fan 160C/gas 4. Remove the cling film from the tray, then bake for 30 mins until the buns are lightly browned and feel firm. Serve warm, sticky-side-up.

NUTRITION:

kcal   731

fat   43g

saturates   16g

carbs 80g

sugars   36g

fibre 3g

protein   12g

low insalt   1.13g

5.   Easy Banana Pancakes

Prep:5 mins

Cook:10 mins

Easy

Makes 12 pancakes

INGREDIENTS:

- 350g self-raising flour
- 1 tsp baking powder
- 2 very ripe bananas
- 2 medium eggs
- 1 tsp vanilla extract
- 250ml whole milk
- butter, for frying

To serve

- 2 just ripe bananas, sliced
- maple syrup (optional)
- pecan halves, toasted and roughly chopped (optional)

METHOD

1. Sieve the flour, baking powder and a generous pinch of salt into a large bowl. In a separate mixing bowl, mash the very ripe bananas with a fork until smooth, then whisk in the eggs, vanilla extract and milk. Make a well in the centre of the dry ingredients, tip in the wet ingredients and swiftly whisk together to create a smooth, silky batter.

2. Heat a little knob of butter in a large non-stick pan over a medium heat. Add 2-3 tbsp of the batter to the pan and cook for several minutes, or until small bubbles start appearing on the surface. Flip the pancake over and cook for 1-2 mins on the other side. Repeat with the remaining batter, keeping the pancakes warm in a low oven.

3. Stack the pancakes on plates and top with the banana slices, a glug of sticky maple syrup and a handful of pecan nuts, if you like.

NUTRITION: per serving

kcal   484

fat   7g

saturates   3g

carbs 87g

sugars   19g

fibre 5g

protein   15g

salt   1.21g

6.   Apple Muffins With Pecan Topping

Prep:10 mins

Easy

INGREDIENTS:

- 350g plain flour
- 25g butter
- 50g dark muscovado sugar, plus 1 tbsp extra for the topping
- 50g pecan , chopped
- 2 tsp baking powder
- ½ tsp bicarbonate of soda
- 1 tsp cinnamon
- 284ml tub soured cream
- 1 egg , beaten
- 3 eating apples (about 140g/5oz each), peeled and cored
- 2-3 tbsp milk

METHOD

1. Heat oven to 200C/fan 180C/gas 6. Line a muffin tin with muffin cases. In a small bowl, use your fingertips to rub 50g of the flour together with the butter to make breadcrumbs. Stir through 1 tbsp sugar and the chopped pecans, then set aside.

2. In a large bowl, sift together the remaining flour, baking powder, bicarbonate of soda and a pinch of salt, then stir in the sugar and cinnamon and set aside. Coarsely grate two of the apples, then beat together with the soured cream, egg and 2 tbsp milk. Make a well in the dry ingredients and quickly fold through the wet ingredients, adding an extra tbsp milk if really dry. Don't over-mix or your muffins will be tough. It doesn't matter if there are lumps of flour.

3. Spoon the mixture into the muffin cases – they should be about two-thirds full – then sprinkle over the pecan topping. Thinly slice the final apple, then poke slices into the tops of the muffins. Bake for 20 mins or until risen, golden and a skewer inserted in the centre comes out clean.

NUTRITION: per serving

      kcal   226

      fat   9g

      saturates   5g

      carbs 32g

      sugars   9g

      fibre 2g

      protein   5g

low insalt   0.56g

7.   Vegan Breakfast Muffins

Prep: 25 mins

Cook: 25 mins

Easy

Serves: 12

INGREDIENTS:

- 150g muesli mix
- 50g light brown soft sugar
- 160g plain flour
- 1 tsp baking powder
- 250ml sweetened soy milk
- 1 apple , peeled and grated
- 2 tbsp grapeseed oil
- 3 tbsp nut butter (we used almond)
- 4 tbsp demerara sugar
- 50g pecans , roughly chilled

METHOD

1. Heat the oven to 200C/180C fan/gas 6. Line a muffin tin with cases. Mix 100g muesli with the light brown sugar, flour and baking powder in a bowl. Combine the milk, apple, oil and 2 tbsp nut butter in a jug, then stir into the dry mixture. Divide equally between the cases. Mix the remaining muesli with the demerara sugar, remaining nut butter and the pecans, and spoon over the muffins.

2. Bake for 25-30 mins or until the muffins are risen and golden. *Will keep for two to three days in an airtight container or freeze for one month. Refresh in the oven before serving.*

NUTRITION: per serving

low inkcal   224

      fat   9g

      saturates   1g

      carbs 30g

      sugars   15g

      fibre 2g

      protein   4g

      salt   0.1g

8.   Monkey Bread

Prep:1 hr and 15 mins

Cook:35 mins, plus rising and proving

Easy

Serves 12

INGREDIENTS:

For the dough

- 200ml semi-skimmed milk
- 85g unsalted butter
- 2 large eggs
- 550g strong white bread flour, plus extra for kneading if doing it by hand
- 2½ tsp fast-action dried yeast
- 50g golden caster sugar
- oil, for greasing

To assemble

- 125g unsalted butter, plus extra for greasing
- 1 tbsp ground cinnamon
- 1 tsp ground ginger
- 1 tsp ground nutmeg
- 225g light muscovado sugar
- 140g pecans, toasted then roughly chopped

For the glaze

- 100g icing sugar , sifted
- ½ tsp vanilla extract
- 1 tbsp semi-skimmed milk
- pinch of ground cinnamon
- 2 tbsp unsalted butter , melted

METHOD

1. Start with the dough. Put the milk and butter into a medium pan and heat gently until the butter melts and the milk is at a simmer. Cool for a few mins, then beat in the eggs with a fork. Mix the dry ingredients in a large bowl with 1½ tsp fine salt, then add the liquid and stir to a sticky dough. Leave for 5 mins, then tip onto a floured worktop and knead for 5-10 mins until smooth and springy. Use a little oil to grease a large bowl, add the dough, turn it in the oil to coat, then cover the bowl with clingfilm. Leave in a warm place for 1 hr or until doubled in size. Knead in a tabletop mixer with a dough hook if you prefer.

2. To assemble, grease a 25cm bundt pan with butter. Melt the rest of the butter in a pan. In a medium bowl mix the spices and sugar plus a pinch of salt. Spoon 2 tbsp melted butter, 3 tbsp spiced sugar and 4 tbsp pecans into the bottom of the tin.

3. Pull the dough into about 65 small pieces and roll into balls. Taking 4 or 5 at a time, dunk the dough balls into the melted butter, let the excess drain off, then tip them into the spiced sugar. Roll to coat, then put haphazardly into the tin. Repeat until there's a full layer of dough in the tin. Scatter with the rest of the chopped nuts, then carry on filling the tin with the coated dough balls. Tip any leftover sugar and butter over the dough. Can be frozen now for up to 1 month. Defrost in the fridge then let prove.

4. Cover the pan with oiled clingfilm then leave to rise in a warm place for 1 hr, or until risen and the dough no longer springs back when you poke it.

5. Heat the oven to 180C/160C fan/gas   4. Bake the monkey bread for 35 mins, or until well risen and golden. Let the pan cool for 5 mins, then give it a sharp rap on the counter. Leave in the tin until just warm.

6. Whisk all of the ingredients together to make the glaze. It will thicken as the melted butter cools. Turn the monkey bread onto a serving plate, then drizzle with the glaze. Let it set, if you can bear the wait.

NUTRITION: per serving

kcal 546

fat 27g

saturates 12g

carbs 65g

sugars 32g

fibre 2g

protein 9g

salt 0.7g

9.   Banana Pancakes

Prep: 5 mins

Cook: 5 mins

Easy

Serves 2 (makes 4)

INGREDIENTS:

- 1 large banana
- 2 medium eggs, beaten
- pinch of baking powder (gluten-free if coeliac)
- splash of vanilla extract
- 1 tsp oil
- 25g pecans, roughly chopped
- 125g raspberries

METHOD

1. In a bowl, mash 1 large banana with a fork until it resembles a thick purée.

2. Stir in 2 beaten eggs, a pinch of baking powder (gluten-free if coeliac) and a splash of vanilla extract.

3. Heat a large non-stick frying pan or pancake pan over a medium heat and brush with ½ tsp oil.

4. Using half the batter, spoon two pancakes into the pan, cook for 1-2 mins each side, then tip onto a plate. Repeat the process with another ½ tsp oil and the remaining batter.

5. Top the pancakes with 25g roughly chopped pecans and 125g raspberries.

NUTRITION: per serving

low inkcal   243

    fat   15g

    saturates   2g

    carbs 15g

    sugars   14g

    fibre 4g

    protein   9g

    salt   0.3g

10. Homemade Muesli with Oats, Dates & Berries

Prep:5 mins

Cook:2 mins

Easy

Serves 4

INGREDIENTS:

- 100g traditional oats
- 12 pecan nuts , broken into pieces
- 2 tbsp sunflower seeds
- 6 pitted medjool dates , snipped into pieces
- 25g high-fibre puffed wheat
- 4 x pots bio yogurt
- 300g mixed berries , such as raspberries, strawberries and blueberries
- Generous sprinkling of ground cinnamon (optional)

METHOD

1. Tip the oats into a frying pan and heat gently, stirring frequently until they are just starting to toast. Add the pecans and seeds to warm briefly, then tip into a large bowl and toss so they cool quickly.

2. Add the dates and puffed wheat, mix well until thoroughly combined, then serve topped with the yogurt and fruit, and a sprinkling of cinnamon, if you like.

NUTRITION:

kcal   478

fat   23g

saturates   5g

carbs 46g

sugars   24g

fibre 7g

protein   17g

salt   0.3g

11.   Easy Banana Muffins

Prep:15 mins

Cook:25 mins

Easy

Makes 12

INGREDIENTS:

- 250g self-raising flour
- 1 tsp baking powder
- ½ tsp bicarbonate of soda
- 110g caster sugar
- 75g butter, melted
- 1 tsp vanilla extract
- 2 eggs
- 2 large ripe bananas, mashed
- 125ml buttermilk (or add 1 tsp of lemon juice to milk and leave for 20 mins)
- 50g pecans, chopped, plus extra to decorate (optional)

METHOD

1. Heat the oven to 190C/170C Fan/gas 5. Line a 12-hole muffin tin with paper cases. Sift together the flour, baking powder, bicarbonate of soda and caster sugar with a big pinch of salt. In a separate bowl mix the melted butter, vanilla extract, eggs, mashed bananas and buttermilk.

2. Make a well in the centre of the dry ingredients and pour the wet ingredients in. Roughly mix together with a fork, being careful not to over-mix. Scatter in the chopped pecans, if using, then spoon the mixture into the muffin cases. Top with pecan halves, then bake for 20-25 mins, until golden brown. Cool on a wire rack.

NUTRITION: Per serving

kcal   223

fat   9g

saturates   4g

carbs 30g

sugars   13g

fibre 1g

protein   4g

salt   0.6g

13. Feel-good Muffins

Prep: 10 mins

Cook: 25 mins

Easy

Serves 6 - 8

INGREDIENTS:

- 175g self-raising flour
- 50g porridge oats
- 140g light muscovado sugar
- 2 tsp ground cinnamon
- ½ tsp bicarbonate of soda
- 1 egg , beaten
- 150ml ¼ pint buttermilk
- 1 tsp vanilla extract
- 6 tbsp sunflower oil
- 175g stoned prune , chopped
- 85g pecans

METHOD

1. Heat the oven to 200C/gas 6/fan 180C. Butter 6-8 muffin tins or line them with muffin cases. Put the flour, oats, sugar, cinnamon and bicarbonate of soda in a large bowl, then rub everything through your fingers, as if making pastry, to ensure the ingredients are evenly blended.

2. Beat the egg, then stir in the buttermilk, vanilla and oil. Lightly stir the egg mix into the flour.

3. Fold the prunes and nuts into the mixture.

4. Divide between the tins, filling the cases to the brim, then bake for 20-25 minutes until risen and golden. Serve warm or cold.

NUTRITION: Per serving

kcal   478

fat   22g

saturates   2g

carbs 66g

sugars   24g

fibre 2g

protein   8g

low insalt   0.66g

14. Pecan Banana Bread

Prep: 15 mins

Cook: 60 mins

Makes: 20

INGREDIENTS:

- 1 cup raw pecan pieces + more for topping
- Cooking spray for coating pan
- 1 3/4 cup gluten free or regular baking flour mix
- 1 teaspoon baking powder
- 1/2 teaspoon baking soda
- 1/2 teaspoon sea salt
- 2 flax eggs or equivalent amount of egg replacer or two eggs
- 1 cup coconut sugar or other sugar
- 1/2 cup coconut oil or pecan oil
- 1/2 vanilla bean or 1 teaspoon vanilla extract
- 1/2 cup plain soy yogurt or regular yogurt
- 3/4 cup ripe mashed bananas

METHOD

1. Preheat the oven to 350 degrees F. Prepare your 9 x 5 banana bread pan by coating the inside of pan with cooking spray and then

sprinkling with a bit of the flour mix. Set aside. In a medium sized bowl, sift the 10 ounces (1 3/4 cup) of the flour mix, baking powder, baking soda and sea salt and whisk to combine.

2. In a mixer attachment bowl, add the flax eggs/egg replacer/egg, sugar and coconut oil. Mix together for about 2 minutes on medium-low speed.

3. Scrape the vanilla bean and add to the mixture. Add the soy yogurt and the mashed bananas and mix everything together for 2 more minutes on medium low speed, scraping down the sides and bottom to ensure everything is combined.

4. Add in 1/2 of the dry ingredients mixture, combine for 30 seconds, and then add in the rest of the dry ingredients mixture. Mix again for another 30 seconds, ensuring everything is combined.

5. Remove bowl from mixer and fold in the raw pecan pieces into the batter until evenly distributed. The batter should be thick.

6. Add the batter to the banana bread pan and use your spatula to smooth down the top. Sprinkle some pecan pieces on top.

7. Bake the banana bread on the top shelf of your oven for 60 minutes, until a toothpick comes out with a few crumbs. You don't want it to come out clean, so watch your banana bread from about 50 minutes depending on your oven.

8. Remove from oven and allow to cool for 10 minutes in pan. Transfer the bread to a wire rack by placing the wire rack on top of the bread, then holding the sides of the pan and flipping it over and removing the pan. Hold the sides of the bread to turn right side up. You can also turn the pan over into your hand, and then flip right side up and place on a wire rack.

9. Allow the bread to cool completely. Slice as desired. Enjoy!

NUTRITION FACTS

Calories 200

Fat 11g

Sat Fat 5g

Sodium 120mg

Carbs 25g

Fiber 2g

Protein 2g

15. Pecan, Ginger and Dried Apple Granola

Prep: 10 mins

Cook: 40 mins

Serves: 18

INGREDIENTS:

- 2 cups old fashioned oats
- 1/2 teaspoon cinnamon
- 1 teaspoon grated fresh ginger
- 1 cup fresh pecan halves
- 1/4 teaspoon salt
- 1/4 cup safflower or pecan or any unflavored oil such as canola or vegetable
- 6 tablespoons packed light brown sugar
- 1 egg white
- 1 cup dried apples, chopped into approximately 3/4-inch pieces

METHOD

1. Preheat oven to 300 degrees F. In a large bowl, mix together oats, cinnamon, ginger, pecans, salt, oil, brown sugar and egg white. Pour mixture in a single layer onto large rimmed baking sheet. Bake for 30 minutes, stirring gently halfway through cooking, to not break up clusters.

2. After 30 minutes, gently stir in dried apple pieces, and bake for an additional 10 minutes. Let cool completely before serving. Store leftovers in an airtight container.

Makes 4 1/2 cups. Serving size is 1/4 cup.

NUTRITION FACTS

Calories 130

Fat 8g

Sat Fat 5g

Sodium 40mg

Carbs 15g

Fiber 2g

Protein 2g

16. Superfood Pecan Energy Bars

Prep : 10

Cook: 30 mins

Makes: 14

INGREDIENTS:

- 15 Medjool dates (9 ounces)
- 1 cup pecan pieces
- 1/2 cup gluten free oats
- 1 tablespoon chia seeds
- 1 teaspoon vanilla extract
- 1/2 teaspoon cinnamon
- 1/4 teaspoon kosher salt

METHOD

1. Preheat the oven to 200 degrees F.

Place the dates in the food processor and process or pulse until they are chopped and a rough texture forms. Then, add the remaining ingredients and process for a minute or so until a crumbly dough forms.

2. Line a baking sheet or jelly roll pan with parchment paper. Dump the dough into the center of the parchment paper and use a rolling pin to roll it into a rectangle that is 6" x 10.5". Cut the dough into 14 bars that are 1.5" x 3" or into a desired shape.

3. Bake the bars for 30 minutes (this step helps to make the texture more dry and less sticky). Cool the bars to room temperature, then store refrigerated in a sealed container between sheets of wax paper.

4. _To package them for on-the-go snacking:_ cut out 4" x 6" rectangles of wax paper, wrap them around the bars, and secure them with tape.

NUTRITION FACTS

Calories 150

Fat 7g

Sat Fat .5g

Sodium 35mg

Carbs 23g

Fiber 3g

Protein 2g

17. Pecan Coffee Cake Overnight Oats

Prep: 30

Makes: 4

INGREDIENTS:

- 2 cups pecan pieces
- 3 cups water
- 1/2 cup + 2 tablespoons coconut sugar
- 1 tablespoon vanilla extract
- 3/4 teaspoon ground cinnamon, divided
- Pinch of salt
- 1 1/2 cups oats
- 6 tablespoons chia seeds
- 1 tablesppon avocado oil

METHOD

1. Preheat the oven to 325 degrees Fahrenheit. Spread the pecan pieces out evenly on a parchment-lined pan and toast for 15 minutes,

until golden brown and fragrant. Set aside 1/3 of the total nuts (a little less than 3/4 of a cup) and add the remaining 2/3 of the nuts to a dry blender.

2. Pulse until a rough pecan flour forms. Remove half of the flour from the blender; set aside. To the remaining flour in the blender, add water, 1/2 cup coconut sugar, vanilla extract, 1/2 teaspoon ground cinnamon and a pinch of salt. Blend until a very smooth pecan "milk" forms.

3. In a large bowl, stir together oats and chia seeds. Pour pecan "milk" over oats and chia; stir.

4. Roughly chop the remaining whole toasted pecan pieces and add to a small bowl with the set-aside pecan flour, 2 tablespoons coconut sugar, 1/4 teaspoon cinnamon, and avocado oil. Stir to create a crumble topping.

5. Store overnight oats mixture in the refrigerator separately from crumble topping. When ready to serve, top the overnight oats generously with the crumble, or layer in a parfait glass. Overnight oats will be ready after 1 hour, or when chia seeds have become gelatinous, and will last in the refrigerator for up to 5 days.

NUTRITION FACTS

Calories 820

Fat 48g

Sat Fat 4.5g

Sodium 25mg

Carbs 91g

Fiber 17g

Protein 17g

18. Pecan Super Seed Crumble Overnight Oats

Prep + Cook: 12 h 15 mins

Serves: 6

INGREDIENTS:

- 1 cup low fat dairy or non-dairy yogurt
- 2 cups reduced fat dairy or unsweetened non-dairy milk
- 1/4 cup maple syrup
- 2 teaspoons vanilla extract
- 2 cups old-fashioned oats (regular or gluten-free)
- 4 to 5 peaches, pitted and chopped

Pecan Super Seed Crumble

- 1 cup pecan pieces
- 1 tablespoon chia seeds
- 1 tablespoon flax seeds
- 2 tablespoons hemp hearts
- 1/2 cup raw pumpkin seeds
- 1/4 cup raw sunflower seeds
- 3 tablespoons maple syrup
- 2 tablespoons coconut oil or pecan oil
- 1 teaspoon vanilla extract

- 1/4 teaspoon ground cinnamon

METHOD

1. _Prepare the overnight oats:_ Combine yogurt, milk, maple syrup, vanilla extract, and oats in a large bowl. Stir to combine. Cover and refrigerate overnight, or for at least 8 hours.
2. _To make the crumble:_ preheat the oven to 325 degrees F. Line a baking sheet with parchment paper or a silicone baking mat.
3. In a large bowl, combine pecans, chia seeds, flax seeds, hemp hearts, pumpkin seeds, and sunflower seeds.
4. In a small bowl, whisk together maple syrup, coconut oil, vanilla extract, and cinnamon. Pour the mixture over the pecan mixture. Using a rubber spatula, fold the maple syrup mixture into the seed mixture until evenly coated. The mixture will be very wet (that's okay).
5. Transfer the granola to your prepared baking sheet. Bake for 15 to 18 minutes, or until golden brown and fragrant. Allow the granola to cool completely untouched. Once the granola is cool, break it up into pieces and place in an airtight container. The mixture will stay fresh for up to

2 weeks.

6. To assemble the overnight oats, add 1/2 cup of the oat mixture to a jar and top with a 1/2 cup of chopped peaches and 1/2 cup (or more, if desired) of the pecan crumble. Serve immediately.

NUTRITION FACTS

Calories 450

Fat 22g

Sat Fat 6g

Sodium 70mg

Carbs 50g

Fiber 6g

Protein 15g

19. Green Apple Pecan Smoothie

Prep: 5 mins

Cook: 0 mins

Makes: 2

INGREDIENTS:

- 1/2 cup pecan milk
- 1 large green apple
- 1 tablespoon maple syrup
- 3 cups fresh spinach
- 10 ice cubes
- 1 tablespoon fresh squeezed lemon juice

METHOD

1. Core the apple and cut it into chunks, leaving the skin on.
2. Place the first six ingredients in a blender and blend. Add the lemon juice and blend for a few seconds again. Taste, and add a touch more maple syrup or lemon juice as desired. Serve immediately, or refrigerate for up to 1 day. Makes 2 cups, large smoothie or 2 small.

NUTRITION FACTS

Calories 270

Fat 18g

Sat Fat 1.5g

Sodium 70mg

Carbs 27mg

Fiber 6g

Protein 4g

20. Maple Pecan Overnight Oats

Prep: 5

Serves: 2

INGREDIENTS:

- 2 tablespoons pecan pieces
- 1/2 cup milk, plus additional splash of milk in the morning
- 1/2 cup old fashioned oats
- 1 tablespoon maple syrup
- 3/4 tablespoon chia seeds
- 3 tablespoons plain or vanilla Greek yogurt *(if using plain, you may wish to bump up the maple syrup in this recipe if you prefer sweeter oats)*
- 1/8 teaspoon cinnamon
- Pinch of sea salt

METHOD

1. Combine all ingredients together in a bowl or mason jar, ensuring all of the oats have been coated in the milk.
2. Cover and place the bowl in the refrigerator where the oats will soak overnight.

3. In the morning, add a splash of milk and stir everything together again.
4. Top with additional chopped pecans, fresh berries, a drizzle of pecan butter or maple syrup, etc.
5. Enjoy!

NUTRITION FACTS

Calories 450

Fat 17g

Sat Fat 2.5g

Sodium 75mg

Carbs 60g

Fiber 9g

Protein 17g

21. Pecan Butter

8 (makes 1 cup)

Prep: 10 mins

Cook: 5 mins

INGREDIENTS:

- 2 cups pecan pieces
- 1/2 teaspoon cinnamon
- 1/4 teaspoon kosher salt

METHOD

1. Preheat oven to 350 degrees F.
2. Place the pecan pieces on a baking sheet and roast for 5 minutes. Remove from the oven and allow to cool slightly.
3. Place the pecan pieces, kosher salt, and cinnamon in a food processor. Process on high speed for about 1 minute until crumbly, then scrape down the bowl. Process again for about 1 minute until creamy, then scrape down the bowl. Process for another minute or two until completely creamy and smooth, scraping as necessary. Taste and if desired, add a few pinches of additional salt and

blend again until fully incorporated. Pour into a sealable jar and store refrigerated.

NUTRITION FACTS

Calories 170

Fat 18g

Sat Fat 1.5g

Sodium 60mg

Carbs 4g

Fiber 2g

Protein 2g

22. Toasted Oat and Pecan Smoothie

Prep: 5 mins

Cook: 15 mins

Serves: 4

INGREDIENTS:

- 1 cup pecan pieces
- 1/2 cup old-fashioned oats
- 1 cup whole milk
- 1 cup whole Greek yogurt
- 2 bananas, cut into slices and frozen
- 3 tablespoons maple syrup
- 1 teaspoon ground cinnamon
- 1/2 teaspoon vanilla extract
- Pinch of kosher salt
- Grated nutmeg, for topping (optional)
- Pecan pieces or pecan halves (optional)

METHOD

1. Preheat an oven to 350 degrees F. Place oats and pecan pieces on a rimmed baking sheet, and bake in the oven, stirring occasionally, until

toasted and fragrant (12 to 15 minutes). Let cool completely.

2. Add toasted oats and pecans to a blender, and blend until finely ground. Add milk, yogurt, frozen bananas, maple syrup, cinnamon, vanilla and a pinch of salt, then blend until smooth. Divide between 2 glasses and top with grated nutmeg and pecan pieces or pecan halves, chopped if using. Enjoy immediately.

NUTRITION FACTS

Calories 390

Fat 24g

Sat Fat 5g

Sodium 80mg

Carbs 39g

Fiber 5g

Protein 11g

23. Honey Pecan Berry Yogurt Parfait

Prep: 5 mins

Serves: 2

INGREDIENTS:

- 16 ounces plain, non-fat Greek yogurt
- 1 cup fresh berries
- 1/2 cup pecan pieces
- 1/4 cup honey

METHOD

1. Spoon 4 ounces of yogurt into the bottom of a wide glass or small bowl. Top with 1/4 cup of berries, 2 tablespoons of pecan pieces, and drizzle with 1 to 2 tablespoon of honey. Top with 4 more ounces of yogurt, 1/4 cup berries, 2 tablespoons pecan pieces, and 1 tablespoon honey.
2. Repeat steps for second parfait with remaining ingredients.
3. Serve immediately.

NUTRITION FACTS

Calories 480

Fat 21g

Sat Fat 2g

Sodium 85mg

Carbs 55g

Fiber 5g

Protein 26g

24. Banana Pecan Cherry Oatmeal

Prep: 5 mins

Cook: 5 mins

Serves: 2

INGREDIENTS:

- 1 cup old fashioned oats
- 2 cups water
- 1/2 cup pecan milk
- 1 banana, sliced
- 1/4 cup pecan halves
- 1/4 cup dried tart cherries
- 1/4 cup honey

METHOD

1. Place oats and water in a large microwave safe bowl. Microwave on high for 3 to 4 minutes or until oats are cooked through. Watch carefully to avoid boiling over.

2. Remove from microwave, stir, and divide between two bowls. Pour half of the pecan milk over each bowl.

3. Divide sliced banana, pecan halves, and dried tart cherries between the two bowls. Drizzle each bowl with 2 tablespoons of honey and serve immediately.

NUTRITION FACTS

Calories 500

Fat 16g

Sat Fat 1.5g

Sodium 45mg

Carbs 90g

Fiber 8g

Protein 8g

25. Berry Pecan Smoothie Bowl

Prep: 10mins

Serves: 4

INGREDIENTS:

For Smoothie Bowl

- 1 cup pecan milk*
- 4 cups frozen mixed berries, slightly thawed (strawberries, blueberries, raspberries)
- 1/2 cup raw pecan pieces
- 2 tablespoons chia seeds
- 2 tablespoons coconut or pecan oil
- 4 to 6 teaspoons honey (optional)

For Toppings

- 1/4 cup raw pecan halves
- 1/2 cup fresh raspberries
- 1/2 cup fresh blueberries
- 1 1/4 tablespoons hemp seeds
- 1 1/4 tablespoons unsweetened coconut flakes

METHOD

1. Add pecan milk, frozen mixed berries, pecan pieces, chia seeds, coconut oil and honey to a

blend and blend until mixture is evenly mixed but still thick (similar to the consistency of soft serve ice cream).

2. Transfer smoothie to a bowl and top with fresh berries, pecan halves, hemp seeds, and coconut. Makes 2 large smoothie bowls or 4 small smoothie bowls.

NUTRITION FACTS

Calories 360

Fat 29g

Sat Fat 9g

Sodium 35mg

Carbs 29g

Fiber 10g

Protein 6g

26. Pecan and Peach Yogurt Muffins

Prep: 15 mins

Cook: 20 mins

Makes: 18 muffins

INGREDIENTS:

- 2 tablespoons pecan pieces
- 2 cups all-purpose flour
- 2 teaspoons aluminum-free baking powder
- 1/2 teaspoon baking soda
- 1/2 teaspoon salt
- 3/4 cup coconut sugar or granulated sugar
- 1 teaspoon ground cinnamon
- 2 large eggs
- 1/4 cup avocado oil
- 1 cup plain lowfat Greek yogurt
- 1/2 cup lowfat milk
- 2 teaspoons pure vanilla extract
- 1 cup (about 2 medium) fresh peaches, chopped

For the streusel topping

- 1/4 cup all-purpose flour
- 1/4 teaspoon ground cinnamon
- Pinch of salt

- 2 tablespoons packed dark brown sugar
- 2 tablespoons salted butter, melted

METHOD

1. Preheat your oven to 350 degrees. Lightly grease a 12-cup muffin tin or line it with paper muffin cups or parchment paper.

2. In a medium bowl, whisk together the flour, baking powder, baking soda, salt, sugar and cinnamon.

3. In another bowl, beat the eggs lightly. Add the butter, yogurt, milk and vanilla. Whisk until combined.

4. Add the egg mixture to the flour mixture along with the chopped peaches and pecans. Fold the ingredients together just until combined. Do not overmix.

5. To make the streusel, combine the flour, cinnamon, salt, brown sugar and pecans in a small bowl. Add the melted butter and mix to form small clumps.

6. Spoon the batter into the prepared tins. Divide the streusel topping evenly over the muffins.

7. Bake for 20 minutes or until a toothpick inserted into the center comes out clean. Allow to cool on a wire rack.

NUTRITION FACTS

Calories 170

Fat 6 g

Sat Fat 1.5 g

Sodium 190 mg

Carbs 26 g

Fiber 1 g

Protein 4 g

27. Spiced Citrus Pecan Breakfast Bread

Prep: 10 mins

Cook: 35 mins

Makes: 14

INGREDIENTS:

- 1/2 cup + 1/4 cup fresh pecan pieces
- 1 3/4 cups light spelt or whole wheat pastry flour
- 1 teaspoon baking powder
- 1/2 teaspoon baking soda
- 1/2 teaspoon fine salt
- 1 teaspoon ground cinnamon
- 1/4 teaspoon ground cloves
- 1/4 teaspoon ground nutmeg
- 2/3 cup coconut sugar or light or dark brown sugar (to taste)
- Zest and juice of 2 oranges (about 1/2 cup juice)
- 6 tablespoons pecan or vegetable oil (such as safflower, grapeseed, coconut, or refined avocado)
- 1/2 cup cold water

METHOD

1. Preheat oven to 350 degrees F. and lightly oil a rectangular loaf pan.

2. In a large mixing bowl, combine the flour(s), baking powder, baking soda, salt, cinnamon, cloves, nutmeg, and sugar.

3. In a medium mixing bowl, whisk together the orange zest, juice, oil, and water. Add these wet ingredients to the dry ingredients and stir until they're just evenly combined (a few clumps are fine). Fold in 1/2 cup pecan pieces. Pour the batter into your prepared loaf, then sprinkle the remaining 1/4 cup pecan pieces on top.

4. Bake the loaf for 35 to 40 minutes, or until the top is golden brown and set. Allow it to cool for 15 minutes before removing the loaf from the pan, then transfer it to a wire rack. Allow it to cool to room temperature before slicing and serving.

NUTRITION FACTS

Calories 180

Fat 10g

Sat Fat 1g

Sodium 180mg

Carbs 22g

Fiber 3g

Protein 2g

28. Whole Wheat Pecan Banana Muffins

Prep: 10 mins

Cook: 18 mins

Serves: 6

INGREDIENTS:

- ¾ c. whole wheat flour
- ½ c. old fashioned oats
- 2 tbsp. ground flax seeds
- 1 tsp. cinnamon
- ½ tsp. baking soda
- 1 tsp. baking powder
- ¼ tsp. salt
- 1 egg
- 3 tbsp. maple syrup
- 2 ½ tbsp. MCT oil or melted coconut oil
- ¼ tsp. vanilla extract
- 1 small very-ripe banana, mashed
- ½ c. light coconut milk (or regular milk)
- 1/4 cup pecan pieces

METHOD

1. Preheat oven to 350 degrees and line muffin pan with six paper muffin liners

2. Combine whole wheat flour, oats, flax seeds, cinnamon, baking soda, baking powder and salt

3. In a separate bowl, mix together egg, maple syrup, MCT oil, vanilla, banana and coconut milk

4. Gradually pour egg mixture into the flour mixture and stir until batter is combined Fold in pecans Divide the batter into six muffin cups and bake for 15 – 18 minutes.

5. Allow to cool and enjoy!

NUTRITION FACTS

Calories 240

Fat 13 g

Sat Fat 8 g

Sodium 220 mg

Carbs 28 g

Fiber 4 g

Protein 5 g

29. Pecan and Veggie Mini Frittatas

Prep: 10 mins

Cook: 20 mins

Serves: 10

INGREDIENTS:

- 1/2 cup pecan pieces
- 1/3 cup thinly sliced green onions
- 1/3 cup diced jarred roasted red peppers*
- 8 large eggs
- 1/4 cup milk
- 1/2 teaspoon garlic powder
- 1/2 teaspoon smoked paprika
- 1/2 teaspoon kosher salt
- Freshly ground black pepper
- 1/3 cup shredded Parmesan cheese (or shredded cheese of any type)
- Butter, for greasing

METHOD

1. Preheat the oven to 350 degrees Fahrenheit.
2. Grease a 12-cup muffin tin generously with butter.

3. Roughly chop the pecans. Thinly slice the green onions. Dice the roasted red peppers.

4. In a medium bowl, whisk together the eggs, milk, garlic powder, smoked paprika, kosher salt, and a few grinds of black pepper. Divide the mixture evenly into the muffin cups (fill them about halfway). Sprinkle the shredded Parmesan cheese evenly into each cup. Then top with the green onions, then the red peppers. Finish by adding the pecans, divided evenly between the cups.

5. Bake for 20 to 25 minutes until golden brown and puffed. (When you remove them from the oven, they'll immediately start to deflate and will continue deflating as they cool.) Allow to cool for 5 minutes in the tin, then remove. Eat immediately, refrigerate up to 4 days, or freeze up to 3 months. They work great as an on-the-go breakfast or lunch, and are good at room temperature or cold (don't need to be reheated).

*Jarred roasted red peppers are usually available near the olives and other canned vegetables.

NUTRITION FACTS

Calories 190

Fat 14 g

Sat Fat 3.5 g

Sodium 440 mg

Carbs 3 g

Fiber 1 g

Protein 11 g

30. Chunky Chocolate Chip Pecan Breakfast Cookies

Prep: 5 mins

Cook: 14 mins

Serves: 16

INGREDIENTS:

- 1/2 cup raw pecan pieces
- 3/4 cups very ripe mashed banana about 2 medium
- 1 3/4 cups old-fashioned rolled oats
- 1/4 cup semi sweet or dark chocolate chips
- 3 tablespoons honey
- 1 teaspoon cinnamon
- 1 teaspoon vanilla extract

METHOD

1. Combine all ingredients in a large bowl until thoroughly mixed. (Note that the mixture will appear slightly crumbly.)
2. Evenly scoop cookie dough onto a parchment paper lined baking sheet using hands to shape if necessary. Press down with the bottom of a

glass to flatten, if desired.

3. Bake at 350 degrees F. for 12 to 14 minutes or until cookies are golden brown. Remove from the oven and allow to cook on the baking sheet for 5 minutes.

4. Transfer to a wire rack to cool completely.

Recipe notes:

1. *Freezer instructions: Once cookies have cooled completely, store them in the freezer in an airtight container for up to 3 months.*

2. *Reheating instructions: Wrap cookie in a paper towel and reheat in the microwave for 15 seconds. Repeat by 10 second intervals if not warm all the way through.*

3. *For a cakier cookie: Add one egg to the mixture for a cookie that has a more cake-like texture.*

NUTRITION FACTS

Calories 90

Fat 4g

Sat Fat 1g

Sodium 0mg

Carbs 14g

Fiber 2g

Protein 2g

31. Pecan Pie Baked Oatmeal

Prep: 15 mins

Cook: 35 mins

Makes: 8

INGREDIENTS:

For the Baked Oatmeal:

- 2 large eggs
- 2 cups milk or pecan milk
- 1 teaspoon vanilla
- 2 cups old fashioned rolled oats
- 1 teaspoon baking powder
- 1/4 teaspoon cinnamon
- 1/4 teaspoon salt

For the Pecan Pie Topping:

- 2 tablespoons unsalted butter
- 1/4 cup packed light brown sugar
- 2 tablespoons pure maple syrup
- 1 cup pecan halves

METHOD

1. *To make the Baked Oatmeal*: Preheat oven to 350° F. Spray the bottom and sides of an 8-

or 9-inch square baking dish with cooking spray.

2. In a large bowl, whisk the eggs, milk, and vanilla. Add the oats, baking powder, cinnamon, and salt and mix well.

3. Pour mixture into prepared baking dish. Bake oatmeal mixture for 10 minutes. (It will go back in the oven with the topping)

4. ***To make the Pecan Pie Topping:***

   While the oatmeal is baking, prepare the pecan pie topping: In a small saucepan over medium-high heat, bring the butter, brown sugar, and maple syrup to a boil. Stir in the pecans.

5. Remove the oatmeal from the oven (after the 10 minutes), spread the pecan mixture over the top, and return to the oven to bake for another 10-15 minutes, until the liquid has been absorbed, and the center is set.

6. Serve warm or at room temperature. Cover and refrigerate leftovers for up to 4 days.

NUTRITION FACTS

Calories 260

Fat 15g

Sat Fat 3g

Sodium 190mg

Carbs 26g

Fiber 3g

Protein 6g

32. Baked French Toast with Pecan Crumble

Prep: 30 mins

Cook: 195 mins

Makes: 16

INGREDIENTS:

For the French Toast

- 1-pound loaf challah, sliced 1-inch thick
- Cooking spray or 2 teaspoons unsalted butter, room temperature (for coating baking dish)
- 4 large egg yolks
- 2 cups heavy cream
- 2 cups whole milk
- 1/2 cup of sugar
- 1 teaspoon vanilla extract
- 1/2 teaspoon ground cinnamon
- 1/2 teaspoon ground nutmeg
- 1/2 teaspoon kosher salt

For the Pecan Crumble

- 3/4 cup pecan pieces
- 2 tablespoons chilled unsalted butter, cut into pieces

- 2 tablespoons chilled unsalted butter, cut into pieces
- 2 tablespoons light brown sugar
- 1/2 teaspoon kosher salt
- Fresh raspberries and blueberries, if desired

METHOD

French Toast

1. Spread out bread on a rimmed baking sheet; let stand overnight.
2. Butter a 13×9" baking dish. Cut bread so slices are similar in size. Arrange, overlapping, in rows in prepared dish.
3. Whisk eggs, egg yolks, cream, milk, sugar, vanilla, cinnamon, nutmeg, and salt in a medium bowl. Pour over bread, pressing bread to help it soak up custard. Cover and chill at least 2 hours.

Pecan Crumble and Assembly

4. Preheat oven to 375 degrees F. Pulse pecan pieces, butter, brown sugar, and salt in a food processor until pecans are coarsely chopped. Scatter pecan crumble over soaked bread.

5. Place dish on a rimmed baking sheet and cover tightly with foil. Bake until warmed through (a knife inserted into the center should feel warm to the touch), 25 to 30 minutes.

6. Remove foil and bake until deeply browned, 35 to 40 minutes longer. Let cool slightly before serving with fresh berries.

NUTRITION FACTS

Calories 300

Fat 20 g

Sat Fat 9 g

Sodium 300 mg

Carbs 26 g

Fiber 1 g

Protein 6 g

33. Extra Sticky Maple Pecan Sticky Buns

Prep: 40mins

Cook: 24 mins

Serves: 12

INGREDIENTS:

Dough:

- 1 cup warm whole milk
- 1 packet (2 1/4 teaspoons) instant dry yeast
- 2 large eggs, beaten
- 4 tablespoons salted butter, melted
- 3 1/2 cups all-purpose flour
- 1/2 teaspoon kosher salt
- 1 tablespoon packed brown sugar

Maple Pecan Sticky Sauce

- 2 cups raw pecan pieces
- 1/2 cup whole milk or heavy cream
- 2/3 cup real maple syrup
- 1/4 cup + 1/2 cup packed light or dark brown sugar
- 12 tablespoons salted butter
- 2 teaspoons vanilla extract
- 1 tablespoon ground cinnamon

- 4 tablespoons salted butter, at room temperature

METHOD

For the dough:

1. In the bowl of a stand mixer, combine the milk, yeast, brown sugar, eggs, butter, 3 1/2 cups flour, and salt. Using the dough hook, mix until the flour is completely incorporated, about 4 to 5 minutes. If the dough seems sticky, add an additional 1/2 cup of flour.

2. Cover the bowl with plastic wrap and let sit at room temperature for 1 hour or until doubled in size.

For the sticky sauce:

3. Meanwhile, line a 9×13 inch baking dish with parchment, and spread the raw pecan pieces in the bottom of the baking dish. In a medium sauce pot, combine the milk, maple syrup, brown sugar and 12 tablespoons of butter. Cook over medium heat until the butter is melted and the sauce bubbling, about 8 minutes. Remove from the heat and stir in the vanilla. Pour the sauce over the pecans.

4. Preheat the oven to 350 degrees F. In a small bowl, mix together the remaining 1/2 cup brown sugar and the cinnamon.

To combine:

5. Lightly dust a surface with flour. Roll the dough into a rectangle (about 9×24 inches). Spread 4 tablespoons softened butter evenly over the dough. Sprinkle the cinnamon sugar evenly over the butter and lightly push the mixture into the butter. Starting with the long edge closest to you, carefully roll the dough into a log, keeping it fairly tight as you go. When you reach the edge, pinch along the edge to seal. Using a sharp knife, cut into 12 rolls. Place rolls in the prepared baking dish, cut side down into the sticky pecan sauce. Cover with plastic wrap and let rise 20 to 30 minutes or transfer to the fridge to rise overnight.

6. Transfer to the oven and bake 20 to 25 minutes, until golden brown on top. If the rolls are browning too quickly on top, cover with foil halfway through cooking.

7. Let the rolls sit 5 minutes and then carefully invert the rolls onto a serving plate. Serve warm and enjoy!

NUTRITION FACTS

Calories 560

Fat 34g

Sat Fat 14g

Sodium 85mg

Carbs 59g

Fiber 3g

Protein 7g

34. Sheet Pan Eggs with Pecan Breakfast "Sausage"

Prep: 8 mins

Cook: 22 mins

Serves: 7

INGREDIENTS:

Pecan Breakfast Sausage

- 1 cup pecan pieces (or slightly toasted)
- 1 teaspoon pecan or extra virgin olive oil
- 1/2 medium onion, diced (about 1/2 cup)
- 1 tablespoon coconut aminos (or low sodium tamari)
- 1 teaspoon sage
- 1 teaspoon thyme
- 1/4 teaspoon nutmeg
- 1/4 teaspoon garlic powder
- 1/4 teaspoon black pepper
- 1/8 teaspoon cayenne

Sheet Pan Eggs

- 12 eggs, beaten
- 3/4 cup fat free or lowfat milk
- 1 cup fresh spinach, chopped
- 1 1/4 teaspoon salt

- 1/2 teaspoon pepper

METHOD

1. Preheat oven to 325 degrees F.
2. *Make the pecan breakfast "sausage:"* In a pan over medium heat, add oil, onion, coconut aminos, herbs and spices (do not add pecans yet). Cook about 4 minutes, until onion is translucent.
3. Add pecans and onion mixture to food processor and pulse until consistency of ground beef, about 8 to 10 pulses. Makes 1 cup pecan "sausage."
4. In a large bowl, add eggs, milk, salt and pepper. Whisk until combined.
5. Add pecan "sausage" and spinach to eggs and stir. Lightly spray a non-stick 12×17 sheet pan with cooking spray. Pour egg mixture onto prepared pan. Place in oven at 325 degrees F. for 18 to 20 minutes or until eggs are fully cooked. Serve immediately.

NUTRITION FACTS

Calories 240

Fat 19g

Sat Fat   3.5g

Sodium 650mg

Carbs 5g

Fiber 19g

Protein 14g

35. Breakfast Bread Pudding with Pecan Crumble

Prep: 75 mins

Cook: 60 mins

Serves: 10

INGREDIENTS:

For the bread pudding:

- 1/2 tablespoon unsalted butter, for greasing
- 1-pound brioche bread, cut into 3/4-inch cubes
- 2 cups milk
- 1/2 cup heavy cream
- 1/2 cup sugar
- 1/2 cup packed light brown sugar
- 1 tablespoon vanilla extract
- 2 tablespoons good bourbon
- Pinch of fine grain sea salt
- 1/2 cup pecans, roasted

For the crumbled topping:

- 1/2 cup flour
- 1/2 cup pecan pieces
- 1/2 cup packed dark brown sugar
- Sliced persimmons, for serving (optional)
- Maple syrup, for serving (optional)

METHOD:

1. Lightly butter a 9 x 13 baking dish, then place cubes of brioche in the baking dish in an even layer.

2. In a large bowl, whisk together eggs, milk, heavy cream, sugars, vanilla, bourbon and a pinch of sea salt. Sprinkle toasted pecans over the brioche, then pour the wet ingredient mixture evenly all over the bread making sure it's covered thoroughly. Cover and let sit in the fridge for at least 2 hours (or up to overnight).

3. **To bake the bread pudding:** Preheat the oven to 350 degrees F. and remove baking dish from fridge.

4. Meanwhile, prepare the crumble: Add flour, pecans, dark brown sugar, cinnamon, salt and butter to a medium bowl, and using your fingertips, rub ingredients together until evenly combined and clumps start to form. Sprinkle the surface of the bread evenly with the crumbs. Bake until the bread pudding is puffy and the top is golden, about 45 minutes to an hour.

5. To serve, cut squares of warm bread pudding, and place on small plates. Top with sliced persimmons and maple syrup, if desired.

NUTRITION FACTS

Calories 510

Fat 24g

Sat Fat 9g

Sodium 420mg

Carbs 63g

Fiber 3g

Protein 11g

36. Pecan Protein Pancakes

Prep: 5 mins

Cook: 10 mins

Serves: 3

INGREDIENTS:

- 1 medium banana
- 2 large eggs
- 2/3 cup rolled oats
- 1/4 teaspoon cinnamon
- 2 scoops protein powder
- 1/4 cup pecan pieces
- 1/4 cup pecan halves
- 1/4 cup maple syrup (optional)

METHOD

1. Add banana, eggs, rolled oats, cinnamon, and protein powder to a blender. Blend on medium speed until mixture is well blended.

2. Heat a large non-stick skillet over medium high heat. Pour 1/4 cup of batter into heated pan for each pancake. Sprinkle each pancake with about 1 tablespoon pecan pieces. When edges of pancake begin to look dry, after about 30 to

45 seconds, flip and cook on second side for about 15 seconds or until pancakes are cooked through.

3. Repeat with remaining batter. Top pancakes with pecan halves and drizzle with maple syrup if desired. Serves 2 to 3.

NUTRITION FACTS

Calories 350

Fat 18g

Sat Fat 3g

Sodium 165mg

Carbs 27g

Fiber 5g

Protein 22g

37. Gluten-Free Maple Pecan Donuts

Prep: 10 mins

Cook: 8 mins

Makes: 12 donuts

INGREDIENTS:

Dry Ingredients:

- 1/2 cup pecan flour, preferably made from toasted pecans* OR 1/4 cup all-purpose gluten-free flour
- 1 cup gluten-free pastry flour
- 3/4 cup gluten-free all-purpose flour
- 3/4 cup granulated sugar
- 2 teaspoons baking powder
- 1/2 teaspoon kosher salt
- 1/2 teaspoon cinnamon

- 1/8 teaspoon nutmeg

Wet Ingredients:

- 3/4 cup buttermilk (no substitute)
- 1/4 cup unsalted butter, melted
- 1/4 cup canola oil
- 2 large eggs
- 1 1/2 teaspoons vanilla extract

Maple Pecan Glaze:

- 1/2 cup pecan pieces roasted (recipe link below)
- 1 cup powdered sugar
- 2 tablespoons maple syrup
- 2 tablespoons 2% milk
- 1/2 teaspoon vanilla bean paste

METHOD

1. Preheat the oven to 425 degrees y. Spray 2 donut pans with non-stick baking spray.
2. In a large bowl, add dry ingredients; whisk to combine.
3. In a small bowl, add wet ingredients; whisk to combine. Pour the buttermilk mixture into the bowl with the dry ingredients. Whisk until just combined (the batter will be slightly thick).

4. Transfer the batter to a large plastic bag (or piping bag). Snip off the corner of the bag and fill each donut cup 3/4 full. Tap the pan on the counter a few times to remove any air bubbles. Bake for 7 to 9 minutes, or until the edges of the donuts are lightly golden brown in   color. Remove from the oven and transfer to a cooling rack immediately by inverting the pan and giving it a gentle tap to release the donuts. Allow the donuts to cool while you prepare the glaze.

5. To prepare the glaze, add powdered sugar, maple syrup, milk, and vanilla bean paste to a large bowl. Whisk until the glaze is smooth and no lumps remain.

6. Dip the slightly warm donuts into the glaze to coat the top half of each donut. Sprinkle each donut with a few generous pinches of chopped toasted pecans.

7. Allow the donuts to cool completely before storing in an airtight container. The donuts are best enjoyed the day they're made but will stay fresh in an airtight container at room temperature for up to 3 days. Makes 12 donuts.

Recipe notes:

Try our roasted pecans recipe.

For the best flavor, toast pecans and make flour by pulsing the cooled toasted pecan pieces in a food processor until it forms a fine crumb.

NUTRITION FACTS

Calories 310

Fat 15g

Sat Fat 4g

Sodium 240mg

Carbs 41g

Fiber 1g

Protein 3g

Printed in June 2023
by Rotomail Italia S.p.A., Vignate (MI) - Italy